P9-AFD-902

WITHDRAWN
UTSA LIBRARIES

WITHDRAWN
UTSA LIBRARIES

MONSTER

MONSTER

poems by Robin Morgan

Random House   New York

Some of the poems in this book have appeared in

The Activist, The Antioch Review, The Atlantic, Caw!, Feminist Art Journal, Motive, Off Our Backs, Poetry Northwest, Rat, The Sewanee Review, The University of Kansas City Review, Up From Under, The Yale Review, Woman's World, and in the anthologies *Campfires of the Resistance, Sisterhood is Powerful,* and *The Young American Writers.*

Some sections of "Four Visions on Vietnam" first appeared in an earlier form in *The Hudson Review.*

Copyright © *1961, 1962, 1963, 1965, 1966, 1967, 1968, 1970, 1971, 1972 by Robin Morgan*

All rights reserved under International and Pan-American Copyright Conventions. Published in the United States by Random House, Inc., New York, and simultaneously in Canada by Random House of Canada Limited, Toronto.

Library of Congress Cataloging in Publication Data
Morgan, Robin.
  Monster; poems.
  I. Title.
PS3563.087148M6 1972   811'.5'4   72-5810
ISBN 0-394-48226-3

Manufactured in the United States of America
9 8 7 6 5 4 3 2
First Edition

LIBRARY
University of Texas
At San Antonio

for Kenneth Pitchford

Contents

I   The Improvisers———3
    Satellite———7
    Eight Games of Strategy———9
    Love Poem———13
    Annunciation———14
    Twins———17
    Quotations from Charwoman Me———18
    Rendez-Vous———20

II Freaks———22
    Dachau———23
    Four Visions on Vietnam———24
    Rebel and Conqueror———29

III Bargains———32
    Matrilineal Descent———33
    The Butcher———35
    Elegy———37
    War Games———39

IV The Invisible Woman———46
    The Summer House———47
    Static———48
    Nightfoals ʻ ———49
    Credo———51
    Revolucinations———53

V   Letter to a Sister Underground———58
    News———65
    The One That Got Away or
      The Woman Who Made It———68
    Lesbian Poem———71
    Arraignment———76
    Excuses for Not Moving———79
    Monster———81

I

Don't sing loud songs,
you'll wake my mother.
She's sleeping here
right by my side,
and in her hand,
a silver dagger—
she's sworn that I
won't be a bride.

—Appalachian folk song

The Improvisers

Crouched by your boots, I look along your body
to that mouth, smiling,
wreathed in the circle of the whip you coil,
but lunge free from your grasp in time to run
unerringly to that other door
the huge woman, the nursemaid,
flings back expectantly, grinning my welcome,
my false safety.
She drags her charge to another room
where the father rises,
black coat, stiff collar, accent, switch, to chide
the daughter pleading she is naughty.
As your hand falls, I scream,
scuttle away to the hall museumed with chains,
belts, sticks, knouts, leather,
past open doors
that expose the sultan's stern command,
the thin schoolmaster's frown, the pirate's anger,
the eluded priest's ecstatic curse.
To the corridor's farthest end
I crawl, to the chamber's center, to the bed
with crimson hangings
I know will muffle all my cries.
Naked you wait,
whip coiled at your thigh, for my demand.

Hours, nights, and years
behind my lidded curtain
—a long, successful run—
I watched my characters

who, scorning their producer,
refused to improvise.
At last, I gave them notice
and locked the theater,

the stage dark ever since.
Only now new actors
hold me by their postures
a captive audience.

I do not know them. I did not call them up.
    But they are rude with indifference,
            stroll a stage-
    street real to the sound of late-night traffic,
calmly light slow cigarettes in doorways,
    and watch for some approaching shape.
        Then you appear, by chance,
windbreaker tight against the cold, and stop,
            ask for a light?
    (I cannot seem to hear the words.)
        Casually you talk,
then you recede together, you and he
    (or they) past any imagined following.
        Sometimes there is a bar,
and a man, untypecast, always laughing
    (I cannot seem to hear the joke)
            your arm around him,
    then your departure, easy, together.
Or clouds of steam, from some dry-ice department
    of my mind, blend and blur
        the movements of you both—

only a line of muscle, a limb
delineated.
But always it ends, and this I fear
more than my rack-suite
or the bed looming behind a crimson shroud:
always it ends with me among them,
too swift to tell
which arms embrace women, which men,
caressing beards, full breasts, until we fall
in pantomime
to that living carpet, some dismembered,
calves haired and soft,
torsos planed unlike a woman's.
Her nails on my breast describe his triangle hips
beside us, narrowed from shoulders that curve
as your fingers mold them. Her hair
brushes my lips as whose hands
widen my thighs,
and mouths open all like flowers
soundless, stroboscopic, slow, to darkness,
opening to the room where you and he
and all of them squirm, then stiffen
oh beyond
my help or hurt or memory.

You curl beside me, sleeping,
unreachable, alien, known.
How can I finish the scene
that betrays me to such waking?

Each night the actors play
this ritual of vengeance:
I murder every stance
by which I watch them die.

Soon I will have nothing
but our own reality. Listen
before I can be heard,
before my voice can reach you through these hangings:
However strange I seem, learn me
at least to the limit
my foreign posture will allow
or lacerate the scrim, risk sight of the familiar.
You love perceptive mourning.
I prefer
even this daily confrontation
with what we never meet
to all you could see, know, love, too late.
Though a reluctant Prospero,
I've buried all my books,
paid and discharged my actors, struck my sets.
Break your sleep and look at me
before their gesturing
reclaims the dark proscenium.
See that I acknowledge you a stranger
but hold whatever I can learn
like your flesh, inside me.

Asleep in our marriage bed,
so I call out, while you
lean through the steaming day
to make certain I am dead.

Satellite

I wonder if I hate him yet.
We lie awake to feign sleep-even breathing
through space that weights the perigees
our separate bodies spin, fearing to burn, burst, crater
such stillness by a word or hand.
I wonder if he thinks I hate him yet.

How can I hate? I am not here
but coasting a moonscape utterly far from him,
light seconds from the quarrel we did not have:
space, water, time, my breasts and blood divide us:
dishes ticking, clocks to be laundered,
even his eyes that know these things divide us.

"We are equal," he says and says. I will write
my poems in indelible ink on the laundry then
while lost buttons roll where green-marbled meat
molds books unfinished, unvacuumed ovaries, self-pity.
Women ought to be born one-breasted or male
or mindless. "We are equal," he says. We find me wanting.

Yet I've patterned and stitched no other man
to lie beside. Effortlessly faithful
I wax toward curves he charts himself
for straying. I couldn't care more. No woman, either, smiles back
sleeping in my arms. Not even
I—not now—lie there. He has no rivals.

I think of others though: of one
whose lunatic footprints on this dust stopped where
she rested her head in a moderate oven;

of one who sorts through drifted years to start all over,
      sweeping out her husband-son
      so that their child might breathe, a daughter, though human;

      of another so young she thought she had time
    to play the woman game, who now must search
      his closets for her own stored clothes;
of the seasoned poets, just divorced, her recipe—
      unwritten poems—still not having
    nourished his appetite. And the showgirl, drawn

      by a mind to learn its gravity
    repulsed books, talk, thought—all but a child.
      My mother got her child, then drowned
the man beneath freak tides, eclipsed herself in me.
      No other course but this then? To thread
    blood trails past clouded windows to a satellite

      where lesbians, eyes streaming sperm,
    rock fatherless daughters on their crescent laps,
      spinsters dance naked, brutalized brides
scrub their nightgowns endlessly. I am unclean.
      I would still sink back to earth, to him.
      I wonder if I hate these women yet.

      Who set me orbiting this bed?
    My two escapes: to kneel before the oven
      or hang his wrung-out love to dry,
each leaving these windows unwashed of that moon—unless
      I turn to rouse his sleepless fear
    with mine. I wonder if he hates me yet.

Eight Games of Strategy

1

He placed the figure on the highest shelf
in his one room, startled to see its shadow
spring at the wall and pose, elongate to
what seemed a grieving for the other's life.
In the dwindling space it suddenly was unsafe
to take the figure down again: the neat
paws begging for their prey, the eager snout
carved to a smile by some deliberate knife
froze on his sight less than the hidden fangs
swelling with what he knew he dare not prove
was poison. Worse, who dare unfurl such wings?
He shut his eyes against the shape, fugitive
through alley dawns, knowing that where he walked
lamian blessings brooded above his head.

2

Strange, but this castle is not foreign to me.
I somehow know the place. I know these halls,
however grand, are where a creature prowls
in search, he claims, of beauty. I can spy
beneath his velvet cloak to where he
wears beast-hide, wherein a blond prince dwells
in turn; within the prince, whose fairness peels
away like wax, a monster, who can free
a new prince, smiling through new monster-jaws.
I shall settle my gown, arrange my lace,
and rest my ringed white hand between his paws.
Although I fear his eyes upon my face
may yet release in me fur, fangs, and claws,
I sense my saving death in such a place.

3

"I am not yours when you are too much mine."
That phrase predicts the pattern of our ruin:
the victim, self-enchanted with her plea
demanding mercy. And the killer's cry.
"You are not mine when I am too much yours."
That credo curses us, orthodox liars
who claim mouth-to-smooth-mouth responses reach
the love who must not ever love too much.
Poised in the spiral stage we mutely pray
for honesty to slit the masks that kiss,
letting us glare the lover in the eye,
recapture what we hoarded as our loss.
Meanwhile I flee, knowing that you pursue
my step, hard on your heels, pursuing you.

4

And did you think we would not still be enemies?
Dared you assume these hands, fouled with the stain
of older battles, calloused with blasphemies,
would raise white flags between your face and mine?
Upon our battlefields the dead grow ripe
unburied. This is a truce, not an end to war.
Even our concourse bears my spoil, the rape
I cannot shield you from, for all your fear,
nor would I care to, knowing my own desire.
Pledge me the same exposure in your eyes.
Such terms at best are temporary where
cadaverous lovers still obscure our way
with grinning halleluiahs. Here is my hand.
Only these corpses show us where we stand.

5

Slivers of ivory like bone petals flawed
open between them. "Oh look, your queen has broken!"
she cried. He watched the fragments on the board
—pale limbs dismembered in some rite forgotten
by dead gods. "My fault," he said; "you could
have trapped my king, except for her. Checkmate,
almost. I'm such a clumsy beast." She smiled
and swept the shards away. "They're delicate
with age. You couldn't help it, I myself
almost wince to touch them. Pull down the shade.
We'll play again, and use my little she-wolf
for your queen. Ferocious? Yes, rare jade,"
she mused; "your move. Here's brandy, if you like.
Your king's in check again. There's still my queen to break."

6

Always, it seemed, we sat out in the rain
or lingered in the snow, afraid to lose
what cold comfort we had found again,
lightning-bared, like a familiar bruise.
Rarely in spring or summer did we touch.
I watched your body's leap against the wave
from where I lay, chilled, longing on the beach
for the warmth of some ice-isolated cave.
Now at this winter's melting, here we sit
silently watching the season's final flame
consume itself with a grace that comes too late
to save us from the crocus. Each year the same
tears surprise my prayer—that we may bring
our blizzard closeness safely through the spring.

7

That every artery your slow spine branches
is for me to prune—all play of sinews
skeletoned, eyes socketed, hips, haunches,
smile, and walnut brain decaying tissues
ripe as my fear that defoliates this midnight—
that what you are is lost to me as if
I never knew you, that even our love's sweat
dries on the skin in seconds: not for myself
I mourn, though you melt through my flesh like a bullet's silver,
sing like a splintered stake green in my heart.
I who enshroud your human shape could labor
to make you immortal, but love that art
less than your waking, dawn-lit, alive, alone.
Why do you lie so still? What have I done?

8

Palaces built above alleys stink at least
as much as one's own breath behind a mask
of jade or fur or skin. Poison and princes
act about the same, and ghouls are comforting
as rhyme when set before an honest void.
My love, such as it is, has better things
to do than play at sonnets or murder,
not that my life's prepared me for much else.
Still, here we are, meek revolutionaries pledged
to overthrow ourselves, a world we made
useless as these white pages without black
ink informing them, and us, how we laugh
in loud terror to see our strategies tested,
whirling together through a chaos indifferent to all
our cries that we have passed the proper point of stopping.

Love Poem

                              that I've never written
simply, without qualifying in some corner
by a careful bloodstreak splashed against
lust-lovely pastel foam—I can risk casually now,
because that once-safe blemish (like a token
sacrifice to no god's jealousy) spread, hemophiliac,
across all sense of balanced order to destroy
my composition's lie.
And only now, free to stand back and gaze
at that impenetrable rust
I see a varicosity so fine
I can look through its fading threads
to where you float and beckon, riding the spray-blue
of an old nightmare's tidal wave
that breaks its bubble against islands
anodyne as torsos beached in sand
cascading through my fingers. Familiar demons frolic
in the orchard of your face, my dear,
more perfect than a prince's death-mask
because you cannot ever know that you exist
this way. I live alone, a woman so far gone
in fantasy as to create out of herself a creature
with whom she lives, loved beyond either of their skill,
a life-work masterpiece spectrumed as white on white,
endlessly unfinished as a

Annunciation

(dedicated to the five men who beat up my faggot-husband at dawn on
Sunday, February 25, 1968)

I don't know you. I didn't call you up,
either, this time, though I was aware
as always, of the restlessness that sent him out
for a short walk,
to give love, perhaps, or to buy cigarettes.

Was one of you his father, violent
with tenderness for that strange particle of yourself
you couldn't understand, but could destroy, at least?
Was one of you his lover, envious
of what you already shared beyond the same male body:
his talent, intellect, art, though not his willingness
to be hated for their use?
Was one of you his closet-friend, passionate
to affirm a love you must have felt
needed affirming, if only to deny it afterwards?
Was one of you an acquaintance, sophisticated
as the cocktail-party man who told him he was mad,
naive, fanatic, and perverted?
Was one of you his brother, bitter
as our 'gay' neighbor whose stereotype-kindled misogyny
consumed even his own pain,
raging to see us try and cross
his/your/my boundaries?

I can't tell anymore. I don't know you.
And this husband I hold in my arms, who is he
who lavishes my lap with such uncyclical
blood? How did this frail farmer's silhouette
fall, a bird-sized sniper, from its nest, brought down
by five grenades' overkill? His narrow eyes are empty.

14

Why does this black flesh I clutch
whimper like some large cat long after
its head has been clubbed five times flat
by dutiful policemen?
I can't tell anymore.
Or would Vietnamese and Panther suffering
be put aside when offered a more basic bond—
to join the five original also oppressed of course
white workingclass American men
in a brotherhood convened to prove each member
capable of beating up a faggot?
I have seen what I have seen.

You are not rhetoric or theories or statistics,
you are real.
Real as the silver Our Lady dangling from the bull-neck
that craned to see the effect of the ten fists
crushing his skull, not knowing, never knowing
that those blows release only more gaudy hallucinations
of freedom rainbowing from his heart
through all your grey matter;
real as his mad poems, his naive love,
his fanatic revolution, his perverted struggles to change;
real as my young husband dying before his murder in Detroit;
real as my boy husband tortured before his execution in Saigon;
real as the rape of faggots by yes look until your eyes weep
red clots of despair the Attica freedom-fighters;
real as his own long hair, his flowing shirt,
his shaven, unmanned face, his smile
that met the fury of your weekend ritual kicks:
to pulverize some hippie commie bastard queer

before speeding off, unlicensed,
back to Queens in time for early Mass.

What are your dreams like, you five?
What do you notice
in your locker rooms, your caucus rooms,
your gyms and bowling alleys?
Whose bodies rivet you
when they smash in lust
on your football fields?
Which thoughts of poolrooms, barrooms, war
most harden you
before, resplendent in sadistic maleness,
you rape "your" women?

I know you. You are real.
I spit this at you, five straight patriotic clean Americans,
and at any who despite whatever else oppression
they have known still choose the luxury
of a united front of masculinist pride:
I will not bear your children, no,
I will not bear you,
whatever line you hand me
for your rapes or revolutions.
I know why you hate strong women,
fear gentle men.
I will abort your contempt, your terror, your babies
by my own hand.
For I am pregnant with murder.
The pains are coming faster now,
and not all your anesthetics
nor even my own screams
can stop them.
My time has come.

Twins

You thought to rest in her,
find sanctuary from your search
of still more years
for him whose sightless gaze,
oiled arms, and visored brain
could kill you or be killed—
or bless, enfold you once,
and make you man:
the vision all your mirrored fragments
dared not frame.

No such silver glaze
shields her image, dull as swift water,
unreflective,
unthreatening as the choice
you braved for her sake: that she warp
and wither in your eyes
the shell she wore to hide you,
now shriveling, splitting,
husked. Inside, an unfragmented fool,
Fool, here I am.

Quotations from Charwoman Me

You never asked to be a master
and God knows (if She would only say so)
that I never asked to be a slave.
Position papers, grocery lists
rain down like ticker-tape on my long-march procession
past where you cheer me on,
waving from the wistful side of—let's admit it—
barricades.

You're tired of living without any joy.
You think you're going crazy.
You need my friendship.
You're afraid to demand the right
to be afraid.
You're trying very hard.
I know that, and you can't imagine
how I wish it were enough.

I need to sleep.
I never asked for this;
you never asked.
Our twenty-five-inch son
whimpers in the night
and my breasts hurt until I wake myself
and feed him.
He never asked for anything at all.
We all want just to be a little happy.

Listen, I see an older me, alone
in some room, busy on the telephone
dialing all my terrible truths.

This thing has never let me live
as we both know I might have; yet I see
this thing can cut me down
on some street or podium tomorrow—
or just let me live, alone.

Our child looks back and forth
from your face into mine, and laughs.
You worry about us, wondering if
something within us has broken.
You hold my body as if it were glass
that will cut you.
I'd stop this if I could, believe me, my beloved.
I'm dying of bitterness.
I love your forehead.
Did I ever tell you that?

Rendez-Vous

I would like to meet you
after our great-great-great grandchildren
are not commemorated as the Ancient Ones.

I would like to meet you
when I can no longer remember
being charred alive as a witch,
when you can no longer recall
being roasted alive as a faggot.

I would like to meet you
when we have both utterly forgotten
what tears could be;
when we will wear no
breasts or penis or uterus,
vagina, testicles,
no beard, no blood.

I would like to meet you
in identically muscular clitorine
large-brained naval-less bodies,
smooth green flesh, pale budshade,
that takes nourishment
only from air/sun/water,
not from any prey.

I would like to meet you
when each can recognize
the ember of this planet
glowing in the eye of the other.

Then
we could speak.

II

The Enemy is permanent. It is not in the emergency situation but in the normal state of affairs. . . . The Enemy is the common denominator of all doing and undoing. And the Enemy is not identical with actual communism or actual capitalism—it is, in both cases, the real spectre of liberation.
—Herbert Marcuse

Freaks

You inhale
      Mexican peon sweat under a migrant sun
and smile
      like an Indian guru gazing at untouchables
to feel
      as the paralyzed veteran cannot
blue pineapple ridges
      burst from anti-personnel fruits
of your brain
      strapped shuddering in electric-shock compassion
leak nectars slowly
      through water torture clogging captured Vietcong lungs
down trellises of bone
      ricketed to driftwood shapes cast up on Bolivian
      mountains
where one cell's mandala
      revolves faster than the ceiling above the abortionist's
      kitchen table
spins out threads
      more accomplished than the suicide handicrafts of a
      Seminole girl
humming into each fingertip
      melodies a black jazz-singer died to sing
and all your suffering gathers itself
      beyond any Puerto Rican twelve-child mother's
      ghetto-numbed conception
of itself into lightning-branched desire
      ungnarled as the knuckles of a masturbating priest
at the tip of which finally blooms
      firework graceful as a midnight bomb
the perfect lotus of unconcern
      whiter than a phosphorus wound in some child's eye.

Dachau

(Note: Es-Samu is a Jordanian frontier village.)

Sweetly the furrows flower red
in geraniumed blood-pits, tidy and fair,
bright as the rain black Newark shed.

The birds sing summer above the head
of the granite Jew whose stone eyes stare
sweetly. The furrows, flower-red,

are neat as the signs for tourists that read
"Exit" here, "Krematorium" there,
bright as the rain Es-Samu shed.

In silence, visitors are led
through rusting gates of August air.
Sweetly the furrows flower. Red

are the cheeks of the children, smooth, well-fed,
the tourist children with golden hair
bright as the rain El Barrio shed.

Bored, impatient, they play hide-
and-seek in the ovens, laughing where
sweetly the furrows flower red,
bright as the rain my people shed.

Four Visions on Vietnam

(These are four original poems extrapolating on images or themes in the work of Pham Nha Uyen, Tu Ke Tuong, and Huy Can, Vietnamese poets. These poems are in no way English versions or translations from the Vietnamese.)

1   The Dead

The night resurrects itself in answer
to my voice that speaks but says nothing.
Has our struggle been for this? so that the dark
like torture, can insinuate itself leisurely
beneath my fingernails, staining me with darkness?
My eyes are open but see nothing
except the night, riding the wings of insects
like a parasite to pollute green earth
that broods on my conscious sleep.
My memory is open but knows nothing
except those crimson peonies rupturing the sky,
except those people whose agony slowly releases them slowly,
whose gasping cracks the earth's heart at last
as they cling to a small windowframe, sliding, sliding.

You who wear guilt like mourning,
embalm your indifference while you still can.
Soon you will be unable to respectfully close
the small barred window of hope
that is ours:
that is open to the sky but sees nothing:
through which you have passed us twenty years' rations
of suffering: through which we reach a fist that grasps nothing:
through which we send a song that sings nothing
you could ever understand—
but which resurrects all of us
you were so certain were invisible.
Fear us.
For now we are.

2   The Vigil

As summer unfurls the snails in their shells,
the fishing boats return to women who must celebrate
their husbands' catch. Such men smell of seaweed.
Her husband hunts different prey, in the hills.

Each morning she sits by the old pagoda
and listens to the schoolbells
and presses the just-buds with the tip
of her finger, beaded with tears,
a hematic dew.
They have put her on posters, plucky, smiling,
standing beside her anti-aircraft gun.
What do they know, fools,
what do they know?

She should write him, perhaps, that she is pregnant.
What to name this child with his almost-forgotten face?
If it is a girl, Napalm.
If it is a boy, M-14 or Shrapnel.
Child she did not want.
Man she did not want.
War she did not want.
They have named her "exemplary
revolutionary woman"—those men who sit
with their feet up on their desks,
those plump men wearing khaki or creased black
pajamas, grey business suits or tie-dyed t-shirts.
Fools, what do they know?

An abortion is not permitted "this late."

Each evening she waits for sleep until dawn.
She should write him, perhaps,
but why? She can watch behind closed eyes,
seeing him joking with his comrades as they praise
the strength of his seed.
He is closer to them
than he ever was to her.
Still, when he returns, she must smile
and serve him tea.
It is reactionary to think otherwise.
It is also against tradition.

But one night she lies curled tightly in no shell,
netted like a gasping salmon that would strain against
all mesh to batter upstream through reddening rivers
toward that mountain source—
and knows who the bells have been mourning,
and knows why she has not written,
and knows that what she never had is lost,
and knows that only some jungle weed blooms, like her belly,
from his corpse,
while red ants speak through his mouth.

3   J'Accuse
Creator of life,
to imprison our souls you built
bars of bone and walls of flesh,
fingers like jolly tentacles,
legs firm as pine trees.
You put the breath of seasons in our throats
and stamped the light of galaxies on our vision.

Our hair secretes subtle perfumes, our heads
nod like graceful carved totems on our shoulders,
calm as a summer lake.
How much wit and craftsmanship you invested.

Yet flies can be found buzzing in these temples,
weaknesses spawning like larvae already
        covering hatched cocoons.
Prison-museums constructed with dirt,
returning to mud around a fossil of pain.
The heart wells acid but the lips cannot release it.
One hand clutches air, the other digs the grave.

Creator of dying,
you who dare condemn those who deny
your private Paradise, you who demand invocation
to pity the scorched leaves, the broken wings,
the running-sore knees scarred with the myth of you;
when you learn at last the mind's horror at the filth
        of consciousness,
when you finally comprehend how many souls, brains, hearts
have dissolved, putrescent, to pay for your name on their lips—
you will be shocked, no doubt, ashamed, and even repentant,
but hardly able to understand,
as you flee from our liberating rage
to some Swiss universe,
and live in exile off our hoarded tears.

4   Warscape

You can wake up at dawn, but she has already chalked
chartreuse swarms of summer on the trees.

You think you see the sun, but the street artist
knows it for a piece of fruit, and so insinuates
onto the citreous sky tart fragrances of noon.

You can plead sanity all you like, but she is mad
and knows how to balance on the edge of trenches,
miming for blind children how to crumple at a burst of fire,
drawing delicate grenades, like beehives, swaying from
defoliated branches; she can outline seared twigs
pointing peace hosannahs toward a phosphorus cloud;
she can show you a corpse in chiaroscuro black pajamas
swinging on the barbed wire. She can even
frown and then complete the composition
with just one touch:
                              a discarded package of Marlboro cigarettes
nearby, the perfect dab of vivid color.

And when your tender dove is pregnant with goodwill,
she can sketch burning villages across your brimming eyes,
cunningly made artificial limbs and pop-art candy bars
for recompense—such kindness truly illumines
all her blackened life; see how grateful she is.

And when you plead weariness at last, and boredom
with all this commitment,
you can return her without fuss to the brothel,
but first let her stroke you a warm autumn garden,
all burnt siennas and umbers, a cosy bed,
and every morning she can tiptoe through invisibly
and add a few more bluish streaks of silver,
as you forget that she exists.

Rebel and Conqueror

(in memoriam Enrico Escobar and Malcolm X)

After so long a siege,
the enemy's tents beyond my walls
have aged as if grown
into the landscape, till they lean like peaked hills
bleached by years of noon.

To refuse without renunciation
and affirm without hope
would seem your only course with a regime
like this one, ordered, rotten, and benevolent.
No revolution ever had a strategy
chiseled from softer stone.

Time, a plumed general,
dined slowly, a guest in his camp.
Spies whispered our shame,
to see a parapet bear the final lamp
for allies who would not come.

All my comrades died,
sliding like stones from crumbled towers—

Unreasonable now, you dare impose
purpose, form
one moment in that officious park, challenging

all alone

its statue, her cold the only audience to your hot speech
till the police sieve your gesture with the sting
of their (at least) concern,

or starving, mad or diseased, behind these doors,
    no flesh warm but mine.

    And my flesh kept awake
    by flies solicitous to churn
      life from dead scars
the siege of days scaled thinly over bone.
    So I outwaited prayers.

    But had the stone warmed and granted
      the state your hand,
    she might only have exposed you as yourself
the victor, victim, spoil; the reconstruction you,
the ruins; yourself the grave cradling yourself the corpse,
    and yours the occupation.

    Still he approaches, demanding
    my name throughout the empty halls.
      I watch, this late,
    rust blossom on his armor as he kneels,
      years, cringing at my feet.

III

You can hold back from the suffering of the world, you have free permission to do so and it is in accordance with your nature, but perhaps this very holding back is the one suffering that you could have avoided.

—Franz Kafka

Bargains

The masks are hung for sale on the pillar,
all four sides.
Not even crowds come to buy them
in the empty courtyard.

> Who sits at the center
> of the great web
> and with one flick
> of one bristle of one foreleg
> sends the universe
> shuddering in orgasm?

The mask is hung for sale on the pillar
they say, all four,
selling them to the night
who buys me.

> Shuddering after I am still,
> the universe loosens,
> tosses me upside down
> to lie exposed at the center
> where I am every strand
> and every fly.

Matrilineal Descent

Not having spoken for years now,
I know you claim exile from my consciousness.
Yet I wear mourning whole nights through
for that embrace that warmed my ignorant lust
even past intimacies you had dreamed.
I played your daughter-husband, lover-son, to earn
both Abraham and Ishmael's guilt
for your indulgence, and in time, reproach.
Who sent us to that wilderness we both now know,
although I blamed you for that house of women
too many years. But Time is a waiting woman,
not some old man with a stupid beard,
and when I finally met my father I found him
arrogant and dull, a formican liar
with an Austrian accent. Well, we meet
the phantom that we long for in the end,
and getting there is half the grief.
Meanwhile, my theories rearrange themselves
like sand before this woman whose flaccid breasts
sway with her stumblings, whose diamonds
still thaw pity from my eyes.
You're older than I thought. But so am I,
and grateful that we've come to this:
a ragged truce, an affirmation in me
that your strength, your pushiness, your sharp love,
your embroidery of lies—all, all were survival tools,
as when, during our personal diaspora, you stood
in some far country blocks away,
burning poems I no longer sent you

like Yahrzeit candles in my name, unsure of me at last
who sought a birthright elsewhere,
beyond the oasis of your curse,
even beyond that last mirage, your blessing.
Mother, in ways neither of us can ever understand,
I have come home.

The Butcher

Poem after poem I had exposed
ogres and virgins in each thought embracing
on dung-fields where mantises swarmed
up stalks of imperturbable flowers;
or how velleity informed even the plainest face.
I had disowned three names and neat conclusions
for what, ophelian and strange,
poem after poem exposed.
So armed, I saw the winter sun
whiten the streets I walked,
crystallize the vomit of holy men
heaped in doorways,
illumine the butcher's lecherous greeting,
the friend's deceit, the infant's colic,
the lover's loneliness.

But the year flaked ice into tears that ran in shame
toward gutters, rushing past where I stood,
blurring the ribs of trees with green.
Vines cracked the sidewalks; matted fur
or feathers medallioned each mating beast.
And, after all, my poems were not prepared
when at last the butcher wiped his bloodied hand
and grabbed my wrist,
when my friend's phone calls
became anonymous, signed only with his breathing.
Afraid, I gave an old bum all my change,
who smiled, then spit at me,
and from his cohorts' cackling
and the gaze of all good passers-by
I fled to my room, but now the baby's demagogic wails

battered against a new door in my brain
inscribed Child Murderer
and I called out—only to find
a weary lover rocking a weary child
and beyond them, our bed strewn
with blood-speckled lilies
hacked whole from the stem of my dreams.

Elegy

After all, the dog was only stunned:
a handsome bitch gulping for air
in the road where a car had left her lying
unmangled, nipples hard with fear.
Her eyes were open, and they knew.

We dream the day's impossible brightness
but wake at night to learn fear-sweat,
an eyeless inquisitor, wheels groaning,
fur, chains, claws, a fog-slick street,
someone lost just beyond awaking.

He will not turn, nor will we wake,
except to lie beneath his wheels,
believing finally that he has passed,
and feel the red in our slackened smiles—
river that widens to no sea.

Insisting death made life absurd,
one man laughed at his torturers
and sped, of course, to his obvious end
in a car loaded with picnic hampers
one invincible summer day in France.

She rose on slim forelegs and fell
back with the rest of her polished body,
nails digging at the pavement to rise
again, trot normally away.
Then the blood blossomed from her mouth.

We read the papers, espouse causes.
Some pray. Some arch in sheeted grace,
willing each membrane to the work
only entropy will enhance.
Some sit very, very still.

The resurrection of the night
each day should teach us how, at least,
eyes watch us clawing, stunned,
for the figure hidden in the mist
breathed by our own mouth's desire.

Sleepwalking dark familiar streets,
we dream the day's impossible brightness
but wake, in time, her sight, his laughter
in effigies anointed to embrace
their only sacrament, our suffering.

War Games

(a mescaline quartet)

1

Creating each other
from unremembered dream-selves past reclaiming,
two men, two women, rise
from separate cells with no more denial
of possibilities they leave behind
to sigh in sleep through midnights of their own unmaking;
with no more denial than feathers flying south feel
for the deserted nest—its unhatched
calculations, fears, reserves left wedged
in the tree's fist now—to metamorphize
only when green crowns those nettles with leaves
lavished for our return. Our.
I will be this one this time, a woman.
You will be he who guides me south,
he whom I carry through the hurricane we breast
wind-buoyed, pinions beating like words to draw the breakers
up across our desert eyes
that watch stillborn components, like sleet-splinters,
foil our hearts and smile
as if that silver could help but fragment before those tides
we settle on to log whole lives through,
seeing murderous driftwood we have carved—this lie,
that fear, this anger, that refusal—
boiled down to sea-shards from once vessels we thought
            we needed
to shudder in above wild water, blind hulks to be foam-battered
toward outlines we cannot recognize but flee from,
cleaving the storm again rather than be broken on
that mast we thought would spine our daily cowardice.
Let it take us then, funnel us inward,

in and up to where the jagged slivers
imbedded in each heartbeat
blur, fuse, bevel themselves into one prism
colorless, virgin, still, until we dare to wake before it
and cast whatever light we have hoarded
on its empty face.

2

She is younger, lovelier, than I ever granted.
A bicycle bear, a dwarf, a clown, I solemnize my carnival self
before her funhouse mirrors. She fears my fear of her.
How could she have known I wore such smiles to kill her?
How could I have guessed the death she deals by being beautiful?
How can I forgive her who at last enfolds me
in the same arms with which I clasp myself?
This ancient rupturing we dance to is a rhythm
older than my own face laughing through her eyes,
moonmark upon us both, Crete calling to Eleusis.
Vines blossom from our nipples, vitreous,
curve and cling along my throat's arch to her hilled belly,
net my hips to hers, our thighs four threnodies
for men unmourned, forgotten, eclipsed by aureoles throbbing
like red moons emblazoned on the snow-sky of our flesh.
We go bare-breasted beneath the cobalt network of our veins;
tiered skirts encircle our mysteries
and amber eyelids imbricate our glance.
We roam the mountains of our rite, keening chants
we never had to learn.
She has four jade arms to gather offerings laid before me.
We have twenty fingers, each lotus-tipped,
knees that have never knelt but grip, grin open, grip

like lungs inhaling into our four mouths the whole world
lost floating in that rictus, until we choose
to give it birth again.

We look across that space to the other, where it stands,
also two-faceted: you and he,
marble and bronze combatants straining against a frieze
of livid action to shatter frail links between metal and stone.
Your buttocks are taut with the force his shoulder sends
in shocks through you, magnetizing your violence with it,
from wrist, calf, columned neck, chest planes, to brittle
back in lightning waves through him,
fracturing, fragmenting, feathering both
until fists unclench and you can use his voice
to name yourself.
Fathers recognize their sons' forgiveness;
Hektor and Achilles break their swords;
Narcissus looks, and lives; Cain embraces Abel.
Humble before your own miracle, gemini,
you are unleaved of all the shriveled whispers
that wilt like spells upon your magic bodies,
free to crumble now, melt
everything within this moment's sap-surge,
move lips to bless salt-rapid floods beneath
this double bridge that leaps across your shores' parallel
to touch a brother.

3
This sudden turning of a corner implodes a glass
I hadn't thought to view again, so filmed from former gazing.

He screens me with my own enmity turned back again,
again, upon myself and him,
an unlearned lesson I dare not feature in his movements.
His indifference glitters like armor.
My fury hacks one breast off, amazon.
Each circles the old positions of the other.
Castrate him or be destroyed. Kill me or be unmanned.
How did I come to be here? What did you need me along for?
Why does he fear *me* and not her?
Why, when she casts sidelong sympathy in my direction
does she counter then with smiles at you and winks to him?
Why do I see slave bracelets encircling her wrists
as she raises her arms to cast off her priestess-crown?
What right has he to patronize my hair?
What right had you to will me here?
Something is familiar, something acrid: my own anger?
A down-draft from the fireplace,
the smell of power, of powerlessness.
Why must I sway to your flashing lights—
I need to see where I am.
Why has she left me for his arms?
            Heartburst:
Why have you left me for his arms?
He will not steal my doubleheaded axe
to slay you with, not while I live.
Hands laid upon me.
They were all lying when they spoke of love.
You needed me there to reassure him
when you touched his body.
He needed her presence to validate being a man.

She needed to do whatever would make him hers.
       Heartburst:
I needed to do whatever would keep you mine.
She cries when I tell her, then denies it.
You are angry and sullen, he is stupidly happy.
Something is burning, the house is on fire.
I understand. I am to be the sacrifice
to this vulgar little man for whom my lover
and my sister long.
Bitter, bitter, bitter this vision.
Hands laid upon me.
It could have been different. It could have been
what I must fabricate out of my own cauterized brain
to survive this reality. It could have been:

4

My hand reaching   Athens falls
your shoulder lifting   the Great Wall stone by stone
her hair falling for Druids to catch and call holy
his foot arching sacred Incan parabolas.
Now the vertical curve has seized us:
our reflections distort at this speed, loom huge,
rush convex, concave, become sound, blur into light
that spills us, four brief children,
through novae bursting lapis lazuli galaxies.
Look, we are stained-glass saints, we are rose and silver,
cerulean and gold. Our haloes' crystal powders
into constellations.
Look, you reach through his hand to touch her heart in my body.
Look, she kisses your lips with my breath from his lungs.

Look, I burn with her melting beneath his weight of you.
Look, he trembles to feel in me your ripples within her.
We are an eight-legged wheel on one pelvic hub.
We spin suns into entropy.
We chip avatars of ourselves from ourselves.
We are biopsied mitochondria, patient scaffolds,
          decomposing vellum
stretched over tissued muscle glazed over dahlian rivers
webbed over vertebrae caged over marrow exploding
peacock, sienna, olive, fuchsia, lilac tastes on our tongues
of flame. Flutes and violins perfume our nostrils.
We hear each other's touch, cinnamon,
twine us, dancing,
up and out through endless universes of the opposite,
through anti-matter, through our own negative,
through she pure he clear you light I energy
we spiral four billion billion millenia
back to this instant, this world, this room,
these bodies, unremembered dream-selves past reclaiming
          —this did not happen—
creating each other.

Ashes rising from the carbon of my heart
          —this will not happen—
and in the morning, a metallic tongue
          —again—
in a dissembling mouth.

IV

I am in Bosch country. . . . I am the creation of my own mind. . . . If the words come, the reality will afterwards?

— Doris Lessing, *The Four Gated City*

Think to yourself, 'I know nothing, I remember nothing'. . . . Let the working tools be as ordinary things that anyone may have in their homes. Let the Pentacles be made of wax that they may be melted or broken at once. Have no names or signs on anything. If you are taken, tortured, and confess, deny it afterwards; say you babbled under the torture. Name no others. If you be condemned, fear not—the Faith is powerful. They may help you to escape if you are steadfast. If you betray aught, there is no help for you in this life or that which is to come. If you go steadfast to the pyre, drugs will reach you and you will feel naught, but will go to death and what lies beyond, the Ecstacy of the Goddess.

— *The Book of Witchcraft,*
written during The Burning Time

The Invisible Woman

The invisible woman in the asylum corridor
sees others quite clearly,
including the doctor who patiently tells her
she isn't invisible—
and pities the doctor, who must be mad
to stand there in the asylum corridor
talking and gesturing to nothing at all.

The invisible woman has great compassion.
So, after a while, she pulls on her body
like a rumpled glove, and switches on her voice
to comfort the elated doctor with words.
Better to suffer this prominence
than for the poor young doctor to learn
he himself is insane.
Only the strong can know that.

The Summer House

Something about that face is unlikable, heavy
with still-firm cheek and pretension,
not even sensual or bored.
Too round, for one thing, like a lewd child's
or incontinent old man's face, chubby, chewing;
a petulant chin, a nose that's coarse and coy,
and pores more prominent than cheekbones.
The lips though, they seem framed
for almost saying something,
almost risking that one kiss before they close
around sleep-fetid breath.
Those eyebrows appear perpetually raised
to arch over sullen lids
cupping more than necessary of the eyes'
attempt to widen in delight at what
they'd wish to squint against in fear.
See how expressions populate that face,
easy-mannered as acquaintances invited
to summer at a country house
which will be emptied at the first slight frost.
Who could believe the owner
keeps, whole winters through,
one caretaker to tend the fire,
except for an occasional spume, a glance
like the signal for despaired-of strangers,
or one untimely guest?
So I was told, at any rate,
when I was there last summer.

Static

Dying faster than usual lately,
I rage to find an ashtray out of place,
a clock unwound, shoes left to stumble over in the dark.
The child must touch each spoke
of the railing but miss each crack
in the pavement, or the world will come to no good end.
Magic faces flicker more convincingly than newsprint
how babies are jellied, generals preserved.
Ashes more fragrant than usual
sift from the mouths of the people I've loved.
The urns are out of place again.
What ceases to tick just before dawn cannot be my heart.
My brain is blank and beautiful
but hide as fragile as curled leather lattices these ribs
that dislocate the day.
Mushrooms grow between my legs at night,
poisonous, I think, but yesterday's broken hours
still lie on the rug, and hungry children swarm
over the unwashed dishes, sparkling iridescent as brown pearl
against my stare. The doors are locked from the outside
like the test-pattern's drone. I've missed some spoke,
some crack is widening like a smile, a door, an eye
flooding blue smoke down my freshly waxed face.

Nightfoals

This one's face
is a pencil sketch alive
in one continuous line
made without lifting the point once.
The nose is exactly like the metal nib
of a quill pen, or a fountain.
Or a sweetheart-neckline on a Thirties dress
worn below skinny collar bones.
There. That was a glimpse of
a dead hunchback's skeleton.
This one must be a bald madwoman.
She's been used before, in *Marat/Sade*,
but she doesn't even know she's a cliché,
and spasms with original horror all the same.
The bedsprings hum in a code I can't make out,
but it's regular, repetitive, insistent.
Medieval lady with your coned hat and veils
beneath your chin,
how can I say politely
that the jewel-clusters of garnet and ruby
fastened at your temples
look like an acupuncture job, bungled?
The man in the World War I uniform and pith helmet
says, "The worst is over." But he adds, "Oh, no,
you can't take that with you."
He means my small casket, I realize,
with the pieces of my puzzle in it.
They never let me work on my puzzle long enough,
which may be kind of them, but I have no way

of knowing that.
Why not me, indeed?
Kenneth was reassuring about the bedsprings, said
they echoed the vibrations from the loud air-
conditioner. He didn't anticipate
that this electric typewriter would be trying
to send the identical message. Deal with that one, kiddo.
Anyway and besides, my puzzle might turn out to be
like Blake's which, when assembled, is a large Io moth,
and the wings of Io moths
have eyes.

Credo

If it is not a Manichean universe.
Of course not.
Still it is true that human limited so-far consciousness
continues to posit only those two basic choices.
Good.
Evil.
And the third—Indifference.
Which is the Ball in the Tennis Game between the Other Two.

the ball isn't bothered, it just sails

Civilizations blaze and one baby
cries, sitting splay-legged in the ruins,

because the Ball is now in one court, now the other.

the Kafka choice.

On what moral right do I dare attempt
to stop the human species from committing suicide?
None.
Especially since suicide is, we all know, the only really
refreshing, new idea with any curiosity about it left at all.

Yet if I care to care
force loving into being, then I pry open

all memory's charnel house of sores
that bubble up eternities of searching for metaphors
that could endure what they were being likened to.

What if I were in neither court, and not even the ball,
but someone sitting alone in the audience, turning my head
first one way and then the other.

So might a schizophrenic sit for forty years,
face poised between shafts of dark and light,
while doctors tried to cure her.

By such will the choice be made.
The mad and the suicidal are the only saints.
The rest of us are merely revolutionaries.

Revolucinations

Can communication communicate only with itself?
This mandala ghost my only reality,
all other shapes, forms, colors I think I see merely
my own hallucinations.
Azure and cherry are the same shade of gold.

Watching with the raptness of one deaf, I see
an old Kabuki woman dancing in sorrow
at having had to sell her only daughter.
Paranoia is the fear of not being God.
A graph chart has many teeth.
Paranoia is the fear of being God.

The windows are shrinking into doors before they vanish
leaving sueded pillars columned like Cretan ruins against
sunsets that ember only into the whoredom of the sea.
None, none of your candles the darkness will not breathe upon.
How could I be caught dead being alive?

A sudden electrical orgasm has flung sequins
in a perfect circle against my eyelids,
nowfishscales unpopulated by fish.
A deathshead appeared out of a white flower last night,
looking in at the bedroom shutters.
I could die tomorrow. The tongue explores the waiting skull
inside my mouth—brief flesh to permanent bone.
I have lived enough
at least, to dare write: I could die tomorrow.
Lies and smiles, my sister said.

Men have forgotten how to love,

women have forgotten how not to.
We must risk unlearning
what has kept us alive.

I think my head hurts
from the fall.
Concussion. Convolution. Convolvulus. Con-
vulsion. Vulva. Velvet. Veil.
Synapses between ganglia and fingertip,
eternally separated from what is beautiful
by the means we employ to perceive it.

I meet my madness in the rosette of a cactus.
I meet my madness in the geometry of a rose.
Why is my madness not beautiful to me?
What are the colors of the lightscreen when the machine is off?
What was my profile before I was born?

He flings her gold bouquets filled with tiny rattlesnakes
flickering their tongues.
Life, they promise, is a terminal disease.

She would go sane again for love of you.
I would even die for love of you.
But what you require is my sanity and her death.

When in life, do as the living.
Lavender hollyhocks are growing from our oriental carpet,
right on up through the chiffon robes of the bloodred Nike
who is waving her arms at us.

He does not even understand
what it is in her he loves.
He does not even comprehend
what it is in her he wants to destroy.
The point, long past, when everything meant nothing.
Now, even nothing has no meaning.

Is a pebble, are a few shells, the sea?
So the few souvenir memories left one after the vision.
But they, like the pebbles, the shells,
are wordless testimony to the myth that the sea exists.

Can transcription transcribe only itself?
Like buds pistillate with the shape of their own death
the revolutionary's ultimate nightmare:
that a voice will echo from the final dark, laughing,
"You have no sister."

—except that, naturally, that would have to be
my sister speaking.

Our time will come.
All hope and all despair in that one sentence.

It's too late for us, my love.
Cling to that wish.

The mask I choose for my madness and suicide
is revolution.

V

We disregard your laws, gentlemen; we set the
liberty and the dignity and the welfare of women
above all such considerations, and we shall con-
tinue this war as we have done in the past. . . . I
incite this meeting to rebellion!
            —Emmeline Pankhurst, October 17, 1912

Do we fully understand that we aim at nothing
less than an entire subversion of the present order
of society, a dissolution of the whole existing
social compact?
            —Elizabeth Oakes Smith, 1852

Letter to a Sister Underground

Dear Jane:

It's funny, now, to write like this:
a letter I don't even dare shape like one
(not that you'll probably ever read it, which may be
the reason it can now be written);
sprawled in a prosy poem
unlike the poems you often asked to see
but which I somehow never brought around.
Well, it's a poem, or non-poem, because
I don't write what I once called poems anymore—
the well-wrought kind that you and I
might once have critically discussed over a gentle lunch
where we were both in former incarnations
"bright young editors."
Instead, I write, or try to, between actions
(which hardly leaves much time but that's okay)
things about women, my sisters and myself
in the hope that some small ticking insight
from the page, which is the one place I don't lie,
ignites a fuse of righteous bitterness
in a woman (my sister or myself)
that can flash into an action no one—least of all me—
could have foreseen erupting.
One thing I know:
there is no atom that is not political,
and poetry can be quite dangerous propaganda,
especially since all worthwhile propaganda
ought to move its readers like a poem.
Graffiti do that; so do some songs,
and rarely, poems on a page.

I should say, though, there's something probably
very "incorrect" here: this non-poem non-letter
ought to go unsigned and
ought to be addressed to Pat Swinton,
Mary Moylan, Bernardine Dohrn, the double Kathys,
and all the other so-called "women underground"—
except that the Women's Movement has taught me
not to be afraid
of being incorrect, and most of all, of being personal.
Some of those sisters I never met at all
and of the ones I know, I know you best.
So fuck it, I'll be personal.

The other point—which is the reason (good as any other)
for this message cast adrift in a bottle sent to
where you never would be anyway even if I did know
where you are which couldn't matter less
is that it doesn't mean one damn disguise
which woman I address this to, or how I sign it,
since all of us are underground.
Each sister wearing masks of Revlonclairolplaytex
to survive.
Each sister faking orgasm under the System's very concrete bulk
at night,
to survive.

Our smiles and glances,
the ways we walk, sit, laugh, the games we must play
with men and even oh my Ancient Mother God the games
we must play among ourselves—these are the ways we pass
unnoticed, by the Conquerors.

They're always watching,
invisibly electroded in our brains,
to be certain we implode our rage against each other
and not explode it against them:
the times we rip and tear at the twin
for what we have intricately defended in ourselves;
the mimicry of male hierarchy, male ego,
male possessiveness, leader/follower, doer/thinker, butch/femme
yes also when we finally learn to love each other physically.
Roles to survive a death-in-life until
that kind of life becomes worthless enough
to risk losing even precious It.

Yesterday, Margaret Mead,
(who was one of my earliest heroes,
for what she learned and wrote about women
in other cultures, for how she proved that we
are not inherently submissive types),
yesterday, in some bullshit seminar
on Women for Peace in Southeast Asia
which some of us had turned into a rap on women and revolution,
Margaret Mead swept in and yelled at me that
women were perhaps so violent that there's
no evidence we might ever stop if we began to kill.
Therefore, the eminent sister had concluded,
this women's revolution must not take place,
we ought not to provoke (dig that) men to be violent
against us, and ought not to unleash our own just anger
at our own oppression. This revolution-talk
in general upsets her: we might be bringing fascism
down upon us—blacks, Latins, Asians, but especially

women, are provoking fascism. My early hero
now writes regularly for Redbook, to survive, no doubt.
Still, she knows, *she knows,*
that women are underground,
thousands of years in hiding, and only now
beginning to surface. Ready.

Our subterranean grapevine, which men, like fools, call gossip,
has always been efficient.
Our sabotage has ranged from witches' research
into herbal poisons to secretaries' spilling coffee on the files
to housewives' passive resistance
in front of their soap-opera screens
to housemaids' accidentally breaking china
to mothers' teaching their children to love *them*
a little bit better than their fathers. And more.
Our rebellions, like the Turkish harem revolts,
have been (as was Nat Turner's) frequent, brave,
isolated one from the other, bloody—and buried,
both in reality and in the history books.
Each time we went into the exile of our women's lives again,
changed our faces and bodies and voices (that's called Fashion),
and passed.
Each time we went back to whispering and waiting.
Each time social change broke across men, we called out,
only to get back each time a reply

rape, beatings, murder, desertion, ridicule, or loving concern

that, in essence, women should be seen and not heard.
At last, when the man has all but destroyed Our species,

Our sister earth, Our children that we made
     in Our own holy bodies,
at last we are beginning to be shrill as banshees
and to act.
To be heard and not seen?
There is an ancient Chinese proverb, long long before
Mao's Quotations, that says
     A man should be careful not to arouse the anger of a woman,
     for he has to sleep sometime—and with both eyes closed.

I remember our ongoing dialectic
(which confused a lot of people—most of all, us)
as it groped its ungainly way toward trust:
you, a "politico"; me, a "feminist";
both of us, after all, just women.
Because what you were really forced to plead guilty to
was the crime of being female and daring to dislike the role.
Because you would be put in a separate prison from the man
you love/hate,
and I am put in the same cage with the man
I love/hate.
Because you once said you knew you were "a mercenary
in someone else's revolution—that of men—
paid with the coin of male approval,"
but that you had to move right now in any way you could,
even if that way was not your own fight
and even if some of your sisters would rather
be volunteers in our own people's army,
whatever that might mean (including everything),
now and later.

Because I mourned that we seemed to have just missed
each other in time—
except that it all becomes whole eventually, you know,
and I look forward to our meeting on the same side
of some totally unexpected barricade, as enlistees of course,
each carrying the one weapon the other most needed
at that moment.

Perhaps it's unfair, or at least indiscreet,
to be saying these things now,
but all's fair in love and war,
and this is both.

How to close such a message?
I miss you.
We are all as well as can be expected.
Hope you are fine and
having a wonderful time.
Don't send a picture postcard when you can.
Stay hidden.
Come back to us.
We'll join you.
Don't accept rides from strange men,
and remember that all men are strange as hell.
Think of us sometimes, my sister.
Forget us, my friend.
Watch for me when you look in the mirror;
I see you all the time.
Take care of ourselves.
See you soon.

In sisterhood, in struggle,
and all that,
but mostly because
I think I love you,

Robin

P.S.: I dreamt the other night
that Blake was *your* baby, whom you'd left
for safekeeping with us.
It's true, you know.

News

1   Bulletins

During the Tet offensive, U.S. marines in Hue
were pinned down for hours by a machine gun "manned"
by an eighteen-year-old girl, who was later killed.
Had she lived, she would not have succeeded Ho Chi Minh.

Indira Gandhi opposed men in both Peking and Washington
to aid Bengali liberation. Yahya Khan had scoffed at her,
"One can't be a Prime Minister and a woman. She is neither.
She must decide." She whipped him.
Ya, Ya.

The April 1972 issue of *Playboy* carries poems
by Mao, reprinted with permission.
Attending ballets, smiling for Nixon, in the wings
of the underground cultural revolution
waits Chiang Ch'ing.

> *Commercial Break*

> The newest homemaker product is *Clean and Kill*,
> by Lestoil.

> The black woman has only one life to live—
> and she is not a blonde.

> The first issue of *MS.* magazine ran full-page ads
> for Clairol.

2   Feature Stories

"The liberation of women must achieve
their total freedom—their inner freedom," said
the husband of ex-guerrilla Alieda March de Guevara.
Che himself had two wives and many mistresses,
as well as making it in the mountains with Fidel
(a notion that disconcerts the Cubans to this day).

200,000 Bengali women, raped by Pakistanis,
have been deserted by their liberated husbands,
who will not touch their now unclean Moslem wives.
Their only options: becoming beggars, prostitutes, or suicides.

Mary Jo Kopechne was said to be an accident.

Only now has it come to light (and scholars all agree)
that Jack the Ripper was a member
of the Royal Family.

3   Sob Sister Human Interest

Kitten and Carmen and Peaches, street whores, know.
They say,
"The Man is white, even when he's black."
They say,
"There ain't no difference. Face it.
Jackie O. sells pussy like the rest of us."

Commercial Break

Be Some Body.

Your face belongs to Noxzema.

4   Editorial

Learn from the nunneries.
Tampons make good wicks.
Let Ethel, Coretta, Jackie, and Betty Shabazz
compare notes.
Oven cleaner or vaginal deodorant
sprayed direct in the eyes
will blind an attacker.

We must all become guilty
of attempted apocalypse.

Is there a recognition any of us know
that can endure itself?
Are we all milkmaids in Marie Antoinette's play garden?

Marie, Marie, let my last weapon
not be taken from me.

Go, unlovely poem,
explode like a mushroom parasol above us,
fuse our fragments maybe,
or at least pop gently into my loosening brain,
and teach me what my own corpse, finally, feels.

The One That Got Away
or
The Woman Who Made It

We all know who I mean, even me.
She is the one who slid like an eel
from knowing any truth larger than herself.
She wheezed orgasms through all her rapes,
married well and joined clubs
and married average and glowed in the perfect home and kids,
and didn't marry but "kept her freedom,"
fucked around in a Virginia Slims imitation of men,
never felt oppressed, of course,
made it into the Senate or
the Weather Underground,
impressed even corporation execs and cookiepattern Che's.
And she took up Zen,
went back to the earth, wore ankle-length dresses
and madonna mystical smiles,
baked natural bread, did astrology
and good works,
got elected to the Board of United Fruit
and the National Welfare Rights Organization Committee,
became a famous artist/engineer/pilot/architect/doctor—
"anyone can, I did; pull yourself up by your own G-string."
She played: matriarch with a sense of humor,
tough broad, fragile flower, spiritual seeker,
Jewish princess, a real pal, earth mother goddess,
tripper, capable unhysterical real woman friend,
juicy cunt, boyish gamin, lyrical lover, chic swinger, and
"your equal"
—and anything else the boys dug in a female
at any given moment.
She even "expanded" her straight consciousness into being gay,
then bloomed into a macho copy of what is easier

to confront in men than in a sister,
of what women in love never meant, not at all.

And yes, we know why.
We can pity the terror and comprehend the threat
to her of a women's revolution.
We can understand that, until yesterday,
there were no other options.
We can even envy the heart-deadening rewards she seems to reap
for placing women last, after everything, anything else.
How she hates us in herself!
How we detest her in our mirror!

And she got herself killed, of course,
trying to shout Black Liberation Now
while her black brother's foot was planted on her throat,
and then took one too many middleclass pills, committing suicide,
and after that had a heart attack at the
Fashion Industry Convention Annual Awards,
subsequently breaking her neck in a ditch, while stoned,
at the free farm in Vermont,
only to get her head blown off in a townhouse explosion,
two days later hemorrhaging out from a safe, expensive abortion,
afterward drinking herself to death or overdosing on smack,
and gave up the ghost forty years later, children all married,
while the other old ladies at the home,
or the entire congregation, or commune, or college, or congress,
or movement, or family, or firm
Felt Her Loss Sincerely.

She refused to understand she was doomed from the start,

and she still doesn't like being reminded.
Too bad, sister.
And there's less and less time for her
to find her own way at her own speed.
She will hide behind our sisterhood, not hers.
She will say this is an anti-woman poem.
She will be the ultimate weapon in the hands of the boys,
And I've just begun to realize
that I must not only destroy what she is,
but if I have to, kill her.

And then cradle her skull in my arms
and kiss its triumphant grin,
and not even cry for us both.

Lesbian Poem

(dedicated to those who turned immediately
from the contents page to this poem)

Thetic:

After centuries of dissecting
Joan of Orleans
as deranged and sexually perverted
objective naturally historians of late
have taken to cleaning up her image.
The final indignity.

It seems, you see, there was a woman
named Haiviette,
with whom Joan lived, loved, slept,
and fought in battle,
whom scholars now say only was
"a girlhood friend"
splashing their filthy whitewash over
what must have been a bed
even Saint Catherine and Saint Brigid smiled upon.

In addition, it would appear
that Margaret Murray, a woman witchcraft scholar,
has found evidence that Joan was Wica, after all.
Did you know that The Maid is traditionally one
of the names that refers to the Coven's High Priestess?
See Murray's *The Witch-Cult in Western Europe*
for further guerrilla news.

Haiviette's name, at last, burns through their silence.
Joan's ashes flicker in our speech again.
Such bones as theirs
rattle with delight

wherever women love or lie together
on the night before
we go to war.

Antithetic:

I love women as a People, yes.
And my breath, work, life (and probably
my death) is bound to women
out of that love.

Yet I have also lain in beds
with some women, yes,
for a variety of reasons—
not the least of which,
surprisingly/obviously,
was male respect.

But if there is a next time, by god,
it will not be for that,
nor will we lie on a plank
in someone's correct political platform,
nor will it be done for abstract female approval
or respect.

It will be because our minds
challenge and delight each other,
and for other qualities I cannot know yet
because they will be hers,
concrete, specific, individual,
like her name.

You can believe it will not be because
she is Woman,
or has honeyed skin
and supple legs,
breasts like pears
and a smell of the goddamned sea.

So get off my back, Sappho.
I never liked that position,
anyway.

Synthetic:

(to Katherine Phillips, 1631–1664, "the matchless Orinda,"
the first *feminist* poet in English who wrote of loving women)

Having come through three decades to where
I will not settle for less than I deserve,
will not long for the past nor compromise the present,
and insist on giving as much as I expect,
I find the personal options narrowed
to the needle of my eye.

To be loved and longed for by a woman
I merely like, but like considerably;
or to be hated by another who really hates
her own most secret desire;
these are not difficult tasks,
only intolerable.

To watch new faces fierce
with single-minded affirmation—
of what is so complex as to have built
on one side of love the bar-scene,
to have dressed women in leather tuxedos
or gingham gowns;
but also to have built on another side of love
forty-year-long enduring pre-fad
marriages between women,
calm and wit-warm in committed dignity—
this task is not intolerable,
only difficult.

To learn to love one's woman-self
has been made to seem both
intolerable and difficult.
To learn to love another woman
in one's self *is* both, and also
worth it.

Meanwhile, she whom I rarely see these years
and I
lay once on separate twin beds
and talked about these very things
through the dark room
until dawn etched sleep on the ceiling.

We must be ignorant.
We only know we may not disappoint each other
and our two lives allow,
as one feminist cell has said,

for no more fun and games.
There is too much at stake; besides, she *is* myself.
We must be wise.

Some of you will be content
with knowing that.

Others will have to wait, forever,
to be satisfied
by the graphic details.

Arraignment

How can
I accuse
Ted Hughes
of what the entire British and American
literary and critical establishment
has been at great lengths to deny,
without ever saying it in so many words, of course:
the murder of Sylvia Plath
?

It should be sufficient to note
the already deplorable controversy
created largely by Plath's own poems and letters
referring to the dear man's peccadillos,
but

her accusation of rape could be conceived as
metaphor,
and besides, it is permissible by law for a man to rape
his wife, in body and in mind.
It is also perfectly legal for him to brainwash her children.
It is no crime for him to malappropriate her imagery,
or even to withhold her most revealing indictments
against her jailor.
It is not illegal for him to make a mint
by becoming her posthumous editor,
and he does no offense by writing, himself, incidentally,
puerile, pretentious dribbles of verse.

Having once been so successful
at committing the perfect
marriage,

one can hardly blame Hughes for trying again.
The second, also, was a suicide,
or didn't you know?
Her name was Assia Guttman Wevil.
He never married her formally—which is no crime.
She translated poems from the Hebrew
and was afraid of losing her beauty.
She is the woman in Plath's poem "Lesbos,"
and, in time,
she chose the same method as her predecessor,
finding the oven's fumes less lethal
than their husband's love.
A Jewish mother in the most heroic sense,
she took her daughter, Shura, with her.
Otherwise, identical.
What a coincidence.
But only paranoiacs would assume
that such a curious redundancy constitutes
a one-man gynocidal movement.

Plath, for example, was clearly unbalanced
for writing such terrifying poems about Hughes.
Guttman, for instance, was obviously mad
for killing her daughter
rather than letting Hughes raise the child.
And I, to be sure, am patently unstable
for thinking both women were sane as Cassandra,
or even for writing this in poetry, rather than
code.

But I am permitted, at least, to
accuse

A. Alvarez,
George Steiner, Robert Lowell,
and the legions of critical necrophiles
of conspiracy to mourn Plath's brilliance while
patronizing her madness, diluting her rage,
burying her politics, and
aiding, abetting, rewarding
her perfectly legal executor.
This is not libelous, merely dangerous, to say.
It is also perfectly legal, you understand,
for publishers to be
men
or cowards,
or members of the same fraternity.

Myself, I have no wish to be ostentatious—merely
effective.

But then, we women change our minds a lot.
That's our prerogative.
So we might not, after all,
free Frieda and Nicholas,
and one night ring the doorbell
to enter, a covey of his girlish fans,
who then disarm him of that weapon with which he tortured us,
stuff it into his mouth, sew up his poetasting lips around it,
and blow out his brains.
Who knows?

Meanwhile,
Hughes
has married again.

Excuses for Not Moving

are
—in number, age, diversity,
and sheer prolific art—
the baroque high genius of the slavebrain.

We are; therefore we justify.

We fear. We know it will not really come
through
personal solutions,
organizing the workers,
picketing, voting, speaking, writing,
living with men, not living with men,
sleeping with women, not sleeping with women,
having panels, speak-outs, speak-ins,
speak-ups, marches, street theater,
learning karate,
or eating natural foods.

We know it will not really come
even from doing all these things
sincerely, for years,
until, as elder eminent revolutionary
feminists, we can pass the flaming
matchstick
on to younger sisters.

We fear; therefore we have reason to fear.

Excuses for not moving
are too myriad to list here.

To even catalogue that ingenious procession
is to spend one's life, successfully,
in hiding.

Excuses for moving, on the other hand,
are singular:
it is fear phoenix in paranoia;
it is despair sharpening itself toward boredom;
it is activity in the process of discovering
energy.

It is what passes through the mist
of all my nightmares:
the axblade, rampant, carved in the profile
of a woman's face.
It is my own unutterable name
which I cannot
yet
pronounce.

Monster

Listen. I'm really slowing dying
inside myself tonight.
And I'm not about to run down the list
of rapes and burnings and beatings and smiles
and sulks and rages and all the other crap
you've laid on women throughout your history
(we had no part in it—although god knows we tried)
together with your thick, demanding bodies laid on ours,
while your proud sweat, like liquid arrogance,
suffocated our very pores—
not tonight.

I'm tired of listing your triumph, our oppression,
especially tonight, while two men whom I like—
one of whom I live with, father of my child, and
claim to be in life-giving, death-serious struggle with—
while you two sit at the kitchen table dancing
an ornate ritual of what you think passes for struggle
which fools nobody. Your shared oppression, grief,
and love as effeminists in a burning patriarchal world
still cannot cut through power plays of maleness.

The baby is asleep a room away. White. Male. American.
Potentially the most powerful, deadly creature
of the species.
His hair, oh pain, curls into fragrant tendrils damp
with the sweat of his summery sleep. Not yet, and on my life
if I can help it never will be "quite a man."
But just two days ago on seeing me naked for what must be the
five-thousandth time in his not-yet two years, he suddenly
thought of the furry creature who yawns through

his favorite television program;
connected that image with my genitals; laughed,
and said, "Monster."

I want a women's revolution like a lover.
I lust for it, I want so much this freedom,
this end to struggle and fear and lies
we all exhale, that I could die just
with the passionate uttering of that desire.
Just once in this my only lifetime to dance
all alone and bare on a high cliff under cypress trees
with no fear of where I place my feet.
To even glimpse what I might have been and never never
will become, had I not had to "waste my life" fighting
for what my lack of freedom keeps me from glimpsing.
Those who abhor violence refuse to admit they are already
experiencing it, committing it.
Those who lie in the arms of the "individual solution,"
the "private odyssey," the "personal growth,"
are the most conformist of all,
because to admit suffering is to begin
the creation of freedom.
Those who fear dying refuse to admit they are already dead.
Well, I am dying, suffocating from this hopelessness tonight,
from this dead weight of struggling with
even those few men I love and care less about
each day they kill me.

Do you understand? Dying. Going crazy.
Really. No poetic metaphor.
Hallucinating thin rainbow-colored nets

like cobwebs all over my skin
and dreaming more and more when I can sleep
of being killed or killing.
Sweet revolution, how I wish the female tears
rolling silently down my face this second were each a bullet,
each word I write, each character on my typewriter bullets
to kill whatever it is in men that built this empire,
colonized my very body,
then named the colony Monster.

I am one of the "man-haters," some have said.
I don't have time or patience here to say again why and how
I hate not men but what it is men do in this culture, or
how the system of sexism, power dominance, and competition
is the enemy—not people, but how men, still, created that system
and preserve it and reap concrete benefits from it.
Words and rhetoric that merely
gush from my arteries when grazed
by the razoredge of humanistic love. Enough.
I will say, however, that you, men, will have to be freed,
as well, though we women may have to kick and kill you
into freedom
since most of you will embrace death quite gladly
rather than give up your power to hold power.

Compassion for the suicidal impulse in our killers? Well,
on a plane ride once, the man across the aisle,
who was a World War Two paraplegic,
dead totally from the waist down,
wheeled in and out of the cabin, spent the whole trip avidly
devouring first newspaper sports pages

and then sports magazines,
loudly pointing out to anyone who would listen
(mostly the stewardesses) which athlete was a "real man."
Two men in the seats directly behind me talked the whole time
about which Caribbean islands were the best for whoring, and
which color of ass was hotter and more pliant.
The stewardess smiled and served them coffee.
I gripped the arms of my seat more than once
to stop my getting up and screaming to the entire planeload
of human beings what was torturing us all—stopped
because I knew they'd take me for a crazy, an incipient
hijacker perhaps, and wrestle me down until Bellevue Hospital
could receive me at our landing in New York.
(No hijacker, I understood then, ever really wants to take
the plane. She/he wants to take the passengers' minds, to turn
them inside out, to create the revolution
35,000 feet above sea level
and return to the takeoff country with a magical flying cadre
and, oh yes, to win.)
Stopping myself is becoming a tactical luxury,
going fast.

My hives rise more frequently, stigmata of my passion.
Someday you'll take away my baby, one way or the other.
And the man I've loved, one way or the other.
Why should that nauseate me with terror?
You've already taken me away from myself
with my only road back to go forward
into more madness, monsters, cobwebs, nausea,
in order to free you—men—from killing us, killing us.

No colonized people so isolated one from the other
for so long as women.
None cramped with compassion for the oppressor
who breathes on the next pillow each night.
No people so old who, having, we now discover, invented
agriculture, weaving, pottery, language, cooking
with fire, and healing medicine, must now invent a revolution
so total as to destroy maleness, femaleness, death.

Oh mother, I am tired and sick.
One sister, new to this pain called feminist consciousness
for want of a scream to name it, asked me last week
"But how do you stop from going crazy?"
No way, my sister.
No way.
This is pore war, I thought once, on acid.

And you, men. Lovers, brothers, fathers, sons.
I have loved you and love you still, if for no other reason
than that you came wailing from the monster
while the monster hunched in pain to give you the power
to break her spell.
Well, we must break it ourselves, at last.
And I will speak less and less and less to you
and more and more in crazy gibberish you cannot understand:
witches' incantations, poetry, old women's mutterings,
schizophrenic code, accents, keening, firebombs,
poison, knives, bullets, and whatever else will invent
this freedom.

May my hives bloom bravely until my flesh is aflame

and burns through the cobwebs.
May we go mad together, my sisters.
May our labor agony in bringing forth this revolution
be the death of all pain.

May we comprehend that we cannot be stopped.

May I learn how to survive until my part is finished.
May I realize that I
          am a
          monster. I am
     a
     monster.
I am a monster.

And I am proud.

About the Author

Robin Morgan's poems have been widely published in literary magazines such as *The Atlantic*, *The Yale Review*, and *The Sewanee Review*, anthologies such as *The Young American Writers*, and feminist periodicals such as *Off Our Backs* and *Up From Under*. This book, *Monster*, is the first collection of her poetry.

A feminist militant who has been active in the Women's Movement since its beginnings, she edited *Sisterhood is Powerful*, an anthology of writings from Women's Liberation, and was poetry editor for the anthology, *The New Women*. Her articles on feminism have appeared frequently and have been repeatedly reprinted and anthologized. She is currently working on her second book of poems, a feminist play, and a prose book positing the next stages in the development of radical feminism. Ms. Morgan lives in New York City.